Let's Play Hide-and-Seek

By Sarah Hughes

Welcome Books

Children's Press
A Division of Grolier Publishing
New York / London / Hong Kong / Sydney
Danbury, Connecticut

Photo Credits: Cover and all photos by Maura Boruchow
Contributing Editor: Mark Beyer
Book Design: Michael DeLisio

Visit Children's Press on the Internet at:
http://publishing.grolier.com

Library of Congress Cataloging-in-Publication Data

Hughes, Sarah, 1964-
    Let's play hide-and-seek / by Sarah Hughes.
      p. cm. — (Play time)
    Includes bibliographical references and index.
    Summary: Simple text and illustrations explain the game of hide-and-seek.
    ISBN 0-516-23111-1 (lib.bdg.) — ISBN 0-516-23036-0 (pbk.)
    1. Hide-and-seek (Game)—Juvenile literature. [1. Hide-and-seek. 2. Games.] I. Title.

GV1207.H83 2000
796.1'4—dc21
                                                                    00-026352

Contents

One, two, three, four, five, six, seven, eight, nine, ten!

Ready or not, here I come!

5

Now I have to look for my friends.

I wonder where they are?

If I find them, I'll race them to **base**.

Do you see anyone **hidden** here?

8

9

Oh yes! There's Jenny!

She was behind the bush!

I'll try to catch her.

I have to **tag** her before she gets to base.

Jenny wins! She yells "**home free**!"

Home free means I can't catch her.

13

Now I have to find someone else.

I see Karen behind the can.

Tanya is behind the tree.

15

I hope I catch one of them.

The person I tag will then be "**it**."

Here I go!

I got you! You're "it."

Now I get to hide.

Go by the base and count to ten.

We need to get a **head start**.

One, two, three, four, five, six, seven, eight, nine, ten!

Ready or not, here I come!

New Words

base (**bays**) the spot from where you count

head start (**hed start**) time given before the game begins

hidden (**hid**-den) to be somewhere that no one can see you

home free (**hohm free**) getting back to base before being tagged

it (**it**) the one who counts and then finds the others

tag (**tag**) to touch a person

To Find Out More

Books

Goldfish Hide-And-Seek
by Satoshi Kitamura
Farrar, Straus & Giroux

Hide & Seek
by Rosella Badessa, John Cast, Roberto Rizzon
Child's Play Internationa

Hide and Seek In History
by Gary Chalk
DK Publishing

Web Sites

Games Kids Play
http://www.gameskidsplay.net
This page has a list of many games that kids can play. Each game has rules for how to play.

Richardson School – Best Games in a Small World
http://www.richardsonps.act.edu.au
Here you can learn new games to play. The rules for each game are given so that you can play right away.

Index

About the Author

Sarah Hughes is from New York City and taught school for twelve years. She is now writing and editing children's books. In her free time she enjoys running and riding her bike.

Reading Consultants

Kris Flynn, Coordinator, Small School District Literacy, The San Diego County Office of Education

Shelly Forys, Certified Reading Recovery Specialist, W.J. Zahnow Elementary School, Waterloo, IL

Peggy McNamara, Professor, Bank Street College of Education, Reading and Literacy Program